Richard Austin's

HORSES
& PONIES

HALSGROVE

First published in Great Britain in 2004

British Library Cataloguing-in-Publication Data
A CIP record for this title is available from the British Library

ISBN 1 84114 398 7

HALSGROVE
Halsgrove House
Lower Moor Way
Tiverton, Devon EX16 6SS
Tel: 01884 243242
Fax: 01884 243325
email: sales@halsgrove.com
website: www.halsgrove.com
see also: www.richardaustinimages.com

Printed and bound by D'Auria Industrie Grafiche Spa, Italy

Foreword

Talent takes many different forms but genius is single minded. That is why I regard Richard Austin as an artistic genius.

Some find the brush, pallet and canvas an entrancing test of creative aptitude and for others, such as myself, photography is an addictive challenge.

Apparently, the camera doesn't lie. Well, it certainly tells me great big 'porkies' on a depressingly regular basis. Reluctantly I have to concede that I lack that extra special 'artist's eye' that characterises the work of truly great photographers.

Richard Austin has that very special rare talent that rises above simple photography and creates enduring images that produce so many different emotions. If you look very closely at Richard's wonderful pictures in this, his latest work, you will discover gems on every page.

As Richard captures the human and animal personalities of the equine world, you will recognise his exquisite talent and understand why I am so grateful that horses, ponies and donkeys play such an important role in my own life.

Noel Edmonds
President, British Horse Society
(and Richard Austin's biggest fan!)

Pepsi squeezes through the legs
of shire horse Gulliver at the
Miniature Pony and Animal Farm
near Moretonhampstead
on Dartmoor.

Introduction

The book is a celebration of the many wonderful horses and ponies alive and galloping in the Westcountry, and of just some of the people who care for them.

Horses are among the most spectacular of earth's animals and they have played a monumental part in the evolution of the modern world since man first climbed upon a horse's back.

Here in the Westcountry we are blessed with more than our fair share of these wonderful animals – and long may it last.

Richard Austin

Acknowledgements

The book is a collection of images that I have been privileged as a newspaper photographer to photograph over the past ten years, and without the help and enthusiasm of owners, trainers and horse welfare organisations this book would not have been possible. My thanks and gratitude to all those who have allowed me to photograph themselves and their animals.
Also a special thanks to the Western Morning News.

The foals at the Miniature Pony and Animal Farm are so approachable, and children love them.

The annual round-up, or 'drift', of Dartmoor ponies brings together the stallions
who do not always get on well with each other.

A pair of foals scampering around a paddock without a care in the world.

Ann Williams with Domino and Lupin concentrating hard on straight lines at a ploughing match in Somerset.

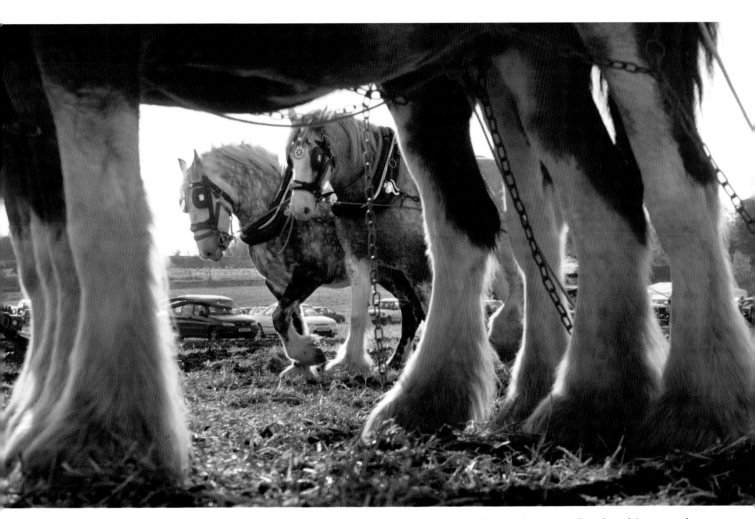

Lining up for a day in the furrows. The big boys of the horse world ready for the start of a ploughing match.

Twin Dartmoor ponies grazing at Powderham Castle.

Humphrey the Welsh pony and Galaxy the coloured horse getting spruced up for the Devon County Show at Oaklands Stable near Exeter in Devon.

Getting the youngsters out of bed in
the morning is the same the world over,
and the Dartmoor based miniature donkeys
at the Miniature Pony and Animal Farm,
Moretonhampstead are no different.

Opposite: The day-old miniature donkey foal
at the Miniature Pony and Animal Farm,
ventures outside for the first time into
the field of buttercups.

Children at Christine Knowles's riding stables have a hobby horse each
to ride and groom as an introduction to horse riding.

Pages 17 and 19: The Kings Troop Royal Horse Artillery on holiday in North Devon at Woolacombe, where the sand and saltwater made a pleasant change from the streets of London.

Overleaf: Sgt Damien Gascoyne MBE rides Henchman through the surf at Woolacombe in North Devon, with Otto his Dalmatian dog. Henchman and Sgt Gascoyne led the late Princess of Wales's funeral procession through London to Westminster Abbey.

Andrew Baynes creates a mermaid and a mer-horse on Exmouth beach.

Opposite: Cooling down the ponies on a hot summer's day with water and beer.

Her name is Chocolate Tart and she is a little miracle horse. Her mother, Madame Percy, underwent a serious operation on her uterus at Bristol University before the foal's birth.

Pip gets a friendly hoof from behind when his friend Trojan wants to move forward.

Kate Mew with her horse
Ladybird (*right*), and with Ferryman
(*above*) in the Equine Therapeutic Spa
at Axewater Equestrian Centre
near Axminster, Devon.

Dundee the miniature pony foal owes his life to his owner Christine Harding
after she helped deliver the foal during a difficult birth.

Victoria Ginsberg shares the moment with a new-born miniature pony at the
Miniature Pony and Animal Farm, Moretonhampstead.

Jim, the barge horse on the Grand Western Canal in Tiverton, giving Megan a lift along the tow path.

Chris Murray at the Devon County Show leads out his magnificent
shire horse Fusilier who (*right*) trots around the paddock
at Pennywell Farm, Buckfastleigh in Devon.

The Devon County Show always manages to provide a horse spectacular including all breeds, shapes and sizes in a variety of sports and displays.

The horsemanship of the Devon Yeomanry being demonstrated to the Duke and Countess of Wessex at Powderham Castle in the traditional sport of tent pegging.

The annual round-up of ponies on Dartmoor, known as the 'drift'.

Opposite: Mary King on King Richard at the Bicton Horse Trials.

A little foal follows his leader.

Emma Bartlett gets a kiss from Peebles at the Mare and Foal Sanctuary.

Top National Hunt jockey Tony McCoy over the last at Exeter Race Course.

The first children's pony race to be held at Newton Abbot Racecourse.

Above: The thrills and spills of National Hunt Racing as the horses gallop neck and neck over the early fences.

Left: Jockey Tony McCoy on Manx Magic winning a Novice Hurdle at Exeter.

Left: Groom Claire Howes on the gallops with Stormy Passage.

Below: An early morning gallop at Rod Baker's.

Left: The famous Desert Orchid in full flow at Exeter Race Course.

Below: National Hunt racing.

Angela Brown washes down race horse Holdimclose at Paul Hosgood's yard.

Opposite: Helen Yeadon with former race horses Gilbert's Girl and Caro,
while Shetland pony, Tish,does not want to be left out of the picture.

Helen and Michael Yeadon's retired race horse yard has an excellent guard in the form of this watchful goose.

Rocky is the best beach donkey in the West. He came first in the Westcountry Donkey Oscars and clearly loves his owner Julie Wibrow, photographed here on Paignton seafront in Devon.

Dartmoor ponies at the annual 'drift' on Dartmoor.

Pages 46 and 47: This little Cornish 'mini mule' has a body like a pony and a head similar to a donkey's. He never ventured far from his mother, Dolly, except when he wanted to skip around the paddock, or when being introduced to Bramble the family dog.

Clover and her new foal
at Judith and Derrick
Llewellin's yard near Exeter.

48

A typical Dartmoor scene with a pony wandering across the moor and her foal skipping ahead.

Sadly, many Dartmoor ponies fall victim to cars on unfenced moorland roads.
Here a foal with a damaged leg is photographed near the popular beauty spot of Haytor.
To avoid such accidents motorists are asked to heed the 40mph speed restrictions on Dartmoor.

Opposite: The same pony foal rests on the grass at Haytor.

Dartmoor ponies at Lower Hisley Stud.

Mare and foal at Lower Hisley Stud.

Perhaps it was the warm breath on its back which gave the cat an expression of satisfaction.

Russell the pup gets the once-over from race horse Some Might Say.

A cockerel (*above*) and a duckling (*right*) attracted the attention of a race horse and Shetland pony.

A delighted little girl feeds the ponies at Crealy Adventure Park near Exeter.

Ed, the miniature pony foal, gallops around the paddock at Crealy Adventure Park near Exeter.

Cranley Matador the British Spotted Horse foal settles
in with his new stable manager, Kate Lewis,
at Crealy Adventure Park.

British Spotted Horses owned by Marilyn Pollard.

Showing off... this Shetland stallion lets everyone know he has arrived.

Derrick Llewellin with Lazy Lemon.

Fiona Chesterton on her first full day out of hospital
following a serious riding accident on her horse
Nothing but Purple.

Inside the stables owned by Nigel Hawke in Somerset.

Miniature donkey foal Topsy
Turvey at the Miniature Pony and
Animal Farm on Dartmoor.

Opposite: Topsy Turvey meets the
children at the Miniature Pony
and Animal Farm.

Founder of the Sidmouth Donkey Sanctuary Dr Elisabeth Svendsen MBE
shows her affection for her rescued donkeys.

Early stroll along the beach at Lyme Regis in Dorset.

Pages 68 and 69: Advertised as 'Texas Ollie and Silver the Wonder Horse' – this highly-polished pair put on a pre-show demonstration for my camera at West Point Arena near Exeter, rehearsing a small sample of the tricks and mutual trust that each of them show.

Silver shows what big teeth he has whilst Texas Ollie checks out Silver's tongue.

Texas Ollie puts his 15.3 hands half-bred dappled Connemara through its routine.

Lift off at Shovern Stud open-day with Appledore
Marengo rearing up, and Matthew McLaughlin
on his Andalusian horse, Caluruso.

Spectacular action at Powderham Castle as yet another knight bites the dust during a jousting tournament.

Lucy Johnson out early on the beach on the River Erme estuary, at Wonwell in South Devon, with her horse Patience, seagulls and the sound of breaking waves.

National Hunt racing at Taunton in Somerset as the horses gallop past St Michael's Church.

The Queen's granddaughter Zara Phillips indicates nine minutes before she is due in the ring at the Bicton Horse Trials, and with a serious look on her face she enters the show-jumping ring.

Zara Phillips competing at the Bicton Horse Trials... a pat on the head for French Willow, owned by her mother The Princess Royal, and flying over the fences on her own horse Toytown.

A horse on a zebra crossing in Modbury.

A horse taxi on the streets of Exeter.

Sue Newton watches over Bertie who she believes was attacked by a big cat near Modbury.
Stories of such attacks made by escaped panthers or leopards are not uncommon in the Westcountry.

Beautiful shire horses in Cornwall; mother and daughter.

Charlotte Green applies sunblock factor 8 to Boxer the shire horse
at Pennywell Farm, Buckfastleigh in Devon.

A scene of days-gone-by with a stark contrast of a traction engine
and shire horses at a Devon ploughing match.

Suffolk Punch High Point William stops for a snack with Carol Brown.

Opposite: Splashing around… Carol Brown on Suffolk Punch stallion High Point William.

Anne Roberts shows off Dartmoor stallion Hisley Cravat at the Lower Hisley Stud.

Racehorse trainer Nigel Hawke at his yard in Somerset.

Marilyn Pollard with two of her award winning British Spotted Horses.

Marilyn Pollard with
her tiny new-born
British Spotted Horse foal.

Yanina has a quiet moment with shire stallion Mascot at the National Shire Horse Centre.

Both shire horses are over nineteen hands and make a superb sight as they gallop across a field in Cornwall.

Border collies Jessie and Megan hitch a ride on the banks of the Grand Western Canal in Tiverton.

For his day job Jim the shire horse tows
the barges along the Grand Western
Canal at Tiverton. Here he's pictured
with his working friends Megan and
Jessie on top, whilst Winnie prefers life
on the ground – with owner Ray Brind.

Walkies… Jim and Jessie decide to go for a walk
– with Jessie taking the lead role.

Topsy Turvey loves all the attention
he can get at the Miniature Pony
and Animal Farm on Dartmoor.

Right: All set for a star roll at Exeter
Cathedral; Cindy from the Donkey
Sanctuary with groom Sabrina Vickery.

Fawn the British Miniature Horse suffers from Ballerina Syndrome on her back legs and walks around on the tips of her toes. Getting to know Syra Bowden at the Mare and Foal Sanctuary, she waits for an operation to correct her stance.